This book is dedicated to all who find Nature not an adversary to conquer and destroy, but a storehouse of infinite knowledge and experience linking man to all things past and present. They know conserving the natural environment is essential to our future well-being.

NORTH CASCADES

THE STORY BEHIND THE SCENERY®

by Saul Weisberg

Saul Weisberg is a naturalist, educator, and mountaineer who worked as a climbing ranger for North Cascades National Park for eight years. He has been Executive Director of North Cascades Institute, a non-profit education organization, since 1986.

North Cascades National Park *in northwestern Washington State, established in 1968, preserves majestic mountains, glaciers, forests, meadows, and thriving animal communities.*

Front cover: Mount Shuksan and Nooksack Tower, photo by Lee Mann. Inside front cover: Thunder Creek Gorge, photo by John Dittli. Page 1: Sitka columbine, photo by Jeff Gnass. Pages 2/3: Mount Challenger and Whatcom Peak, photo by Pat O'Hara.

Edited by Mary Lu Moore. Book design by K. C. DenDooven.

Third Printing, 1997

The North Cascades provide a place where people can
experience nature on her own terms, a place where
the artifacts of modern technological civilization fall away.
We are left standing alone, just below the summit,
mist rising from the forest below; before us there is nothing.

K. C. DEN DOOVEN

Tucked away in the northwest corner of Washington State lies a vast, rugged wilderness of rock and ice and snow. Jagged spires and sheer cliffs rise from deep glacial valleys choked with a dense evergreen jungle. Snowy glaciers cling to the precipitous flanks of the peaks, giving birth to powerful rivers that carve their way to the sea. Only 30 miles from the lowland forests and rocky shores of Puget Sound, the North Cascades rise in twisted and convoluted majesty to heights of 8,000 and 10,000 feet. Nowhere else can one find such a contrast of shapes and forms than in these wilderness mountains of the Pacific Northwest.

Taking the full brunt of ocean storms, the North Cascades are alive with movement, life, and power. Mighty glaciers tear at the peaks. Pools of melting snow percolate through meadows on their passage to rivers far below. Rivers and creeks form cascading waterfalls that flow through the forests like the mountains' lifeblood. Majestic cedars stand sentinel in lowlands covered with drifting clouds. High above the trees,

Looking south into the heart of the North Cascades, an alpine world of rock and ice.

subalpine meadows are covered with a carpet of wildflowers, while the alpine ridgetops are home to twisted krummholz trees.

Traditionally a home for native peoples of the Skagit and Chelan valleys who hunted and fished here, this rugged land defied white exploration and settlement for many years. A glance at the map shows names that reflect the experience of the early explorers of the North Cascades: Mount Fury, Mount Challenger, Mount Despair, Forbidden Peak, Mount Torment, Eldorado Peak. Only the lure of gold, furs, timber, and later, hydroelectric power, led to the opening of this vast wilderness. Subsequent visitors came to explore, hike, and climb through the mountains known as the American Alps. Today the land remains wild—much of it protected as a wilderness park—preserved as a place to experience the raw power of creation. It is a place to feel a sense of solitude and to experience the land on its own terms.

A Land of Wild Mountains

The Cascade Mountains, stretching northward for 500 miles from Mount Shasta in California to the Fraser River in British Columbia, reach their greatest development in northwestern Washington. Here the range reaches an average elevation of nearly 7,000 feet and stretches 70 miles along the Canadian border. The Fraser River separates the Cascades from the Coast Mountains of British Columbia. To the west lie the lowlands of Puget Sound, while to the east the Okanogan (o·ka·NOG·an) Highlands and the Columbia River mark the boundary of the range. To the south, Snoqualmie Pass is the dividing point between the older granitic and metamorphic rocks of the North Cascades and the younger volcanic and sedimentary rocks of the southern Cascades.

North Cascades National Park and the surrounding national forest and wilderness areas are the heart of the North Cascades range. Covered with gleaming mantles of ice, two young volcanoes—Glacier Peak to the south and Mount Baker to the west—rise to 10,000 feet. Most of the major valleys within the North Cascades have been glaciated within the last 22,000 years. These valleys now contain the mighty rivers of the Nooksack, Skagit (SKA·jit), and Stehekin (Ste·HEE·kin).

From any of its many summits the North Cascades appear as a sea of mountains, an ocean of breaking waves frozen into spectacular shapes and forms. Glaciers tumble from the higher peaks. Sharp spires and jagged ridges twist from summit to summit, then abruptly plunge into one of the many steep U-shaped valleys below.

This is a range of great beauty, containing some of the most spectacular scenery and complex geology in North America. The geologic history of the North Cascades is an immense jigsaw puzzle—one that is only slowly being pieced together today. It is difficult to study the geologic history of the North Cascades because of the rugged and remote terrain and the vegetation that covers the rock as thickly as green fur.

WATER, ICE, AND JAGGED PEAKS

Water, ice, and jagged peaks are the essence of the North Cascades landscape. Its dominant

Mount Torment rises above the lush meadows of Boston Basin. The rocky debris piles are lateral moraines which show the retreat of the Taboo Glacier in recent years.

PAT O'HARA

Steep north-facing walls rise above Luna Cirque the northern Picket Range. The jagged towers Mount Terror and Crescent Creek Spires loom behin

Crystalline fragments of white quartz intrude on the broken face of this granodiorite boulder, suggesting the ancient writing of the earth.

The convolutions and twisting visible in this Skagit gneiss show the powerful forces at work deep in the earth when this metamorphic rock was formed.

topographic characteristics are near-vertical cirque (SURK) headwalls and steep glacial valleys. Indeed, the North Cascades contain most of the glaciers of the United States outside of Alaska. Even though the 8,000-foot elevation of the higher summits seems low in comparison to the 14,000-foot giants of the Rocky Mountains or the Sierra Nevada, the base of the North Cascades lies close to sea level; vertical relief is as great, or greater, than in any other range. These are steep mountains—often ascending more than 5,000 feet from valley to summit. This amazing elevational gradient makes other mountains seem gentle by comparison.

The mountains we see, spectacular though they are, represent only the most recent, and in many cases one of the mildest, in a series of mountain-building episodes that have occurred here. Before discussing the episodes of mountain

building that created the North Cascades, we must first review some basics about rocks and their origins.

There are three major types of rocks that make up the earth. *Igneous* rocks are formed by the solidification of melted rock, *magma,* or lava. If the magma cools slowly in the depths of the earth, the rocks are called plutonic; granites or diorites (DIE·or·ites) are common types. If the melt cools rapidly on the surface, the resulting rock is volcanic—basalt and andesite are typical. *Sedimentary* rocks are derived, as the name implies, from sediments—from mineral and organic material that has been deposited on the surface, then buried and compressed into rock strata. Typical sedimentary rocks include sandstones, shales, and cherts. *Metamorphic* rocks, such as slates, schists, and gneisses (NICE·es) have been altered by extremes of temperature and pressure below

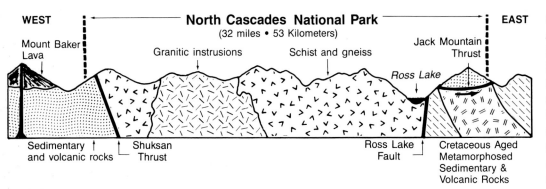

WEST   **North Cascades National Park**   **EAST**
(32 miles • 53 Kilometers)

Mount Baker Lava

Granitic instrusions

Schist and gneiss

Jack Mountain Thrust

Ross Lake

Sedimentary and volcanic rocks

Shuksan Thrust

Ross Lake Fault

Cretaceous Aged Metamorphosed Sedimentary & Volcanic Rocks

Geologic cross section of the North Cascades looking north into the crystalline core of the range. Granitic intrusions caused faulting and metamorphism of adjacent rock bodies.

Davis Peak rises above the emerald-green waters of Diablo Lake, the middle of three lakes along the Skagit River. The reservoir, formed by the impounded waters of the Skagit River at Diablo Dam, provides year-round fishing and boating opportunities. The green color is due to suspended microscopic mineral particles ground from the rocks by glaciers high in the mountains and carried down in thousands of rushing streams.

LARRY BURTON

the surface of the earth. Originally sedimentary or igneous, metamorphic rocks have been recrystallized and deformed by the great temperatures and pressures to which they have been subjected.

The North Cascades are composed largely of volcanic rocks and the sediments derived from erosion of the volcanoes. Intrusive granitic rocks and metamorphic rocks are also prevalent. Volcanism and metamorphism have had a much more important role here than in the Rocky Mountains or the Sierra Nevada.

The central core of the North Cascades contains the oldest and most severely metamorphosed rocks. The crystalline rocks in the range core

(schists, gneisses, and granites) comprise the backbone of the North Cascades. These rocks are mainly older than 60 million years and can be seen along the Skagit River from State Route 20 east of Marblemount. The oldest rocks are gneisses. Most of the intrusions, which are found throughout the range, are composed of granodiorite and quartz diorite. Granodiorite outcrops, such as those that occur in the northern Picket Range, attract mountaineers in search of challenging climbs on the steep, firm rock.

Two different episodes of mountain building were involved in the creation of the North Cascades. Geologists have discovered that the earth's

KEITH GUNNAR

lithosphere, or crust, which floats on the mantle, is composed of large *tectonic* plates that are moving slowly—sometimes sliding past each other and sometimes colliding. The lithosphere under the ocean is composed of basalt and other dense igneous rocks. The continental crust is composed primarily of less dense granitic rock. The northwest-trending structures of the older rocks of the range are thought by some geologists to have been produced by the collision of a small tectonic plate with the margin of western North America about 90 million years ago. This collision probably occurred far to the south, in the vicinity of what is now Baja California. Part of the microplate, which continued to move north, is represented today by Vancouver Island and the Queen Charlotte Islands of British Columbia; the rest of the plate ended up in Alaska.

The north/south–trending, younger rocks of the entire Cascade Range were created in a different way. The Juan de Fuca plate, which lies off the coast, is presently being *subducted,* that is, drawn below the continental margin of the Pacific Northwest. For the past 40 million years this interaction between oceanic and continental plates has caused volcanism and mountain building. Within the recent past (five to six million years) there has been uplifting, or mountain building, along a north-south axis, with the greatest uplift along the Canadian border. In the northern part of the range most of the younger volcanic rocks have been stripped away by erosion, exposing the older, underlying rocks. In the North

Cascades very young (less than one million years) volcanoes like Glacier Peak and Mount Baker have been constructed atop rocks that are hundreds of millions of years old.

The North Cascades were built over hundreds of millions of years by the accumulation of sediments deposited in ancient seas, by the collision of tectonic plates and the metamorphism produced by the collision, and, finally, by the upwelling of molten magma and the rising of bedrock that displaced the ocean to the west. The mountains we see today have resulted from the recent uplift of the ancient rocks and erosion of the surface of the land. The volcanoes are a spectacular and last-minute addition to the story. In the past few million years the uplift in the northern end of the range has continued. Volcanism, glaciation, and stream erosion continue to play the major roles in creating the landscape.

Rivers of Water, Rivers of Ice

The powers that raise mountains are folding, faulting, and volcanism. In opposition are the erosional forces of water in rain, streams and rivers, and glaciers that literally tear down the mountains. Glaciation is especially prominent in the North Cascades. The craggy summits of the high peaks and the deep U-shaped valleys are both due to glacial erosion.

Glaciers are moving masses of ice formed by the compaction and recrystallization of snow. Alpine glaciers originate in an *accumulation zone* where the rate of snowfall is great. For a glacier to form, more snow must fall each year than is lost by melting and evaporation. The immense weight of ice accumulated over many years causes the ice to move downhill. The glacier flows downslope to a point known as the snout, or terminus,

Tumbling from a gentle gradient above, the Challenger Glacier plunges steeply over a hidden break between vertical rock walls. The small glacial tarn was formed by the retreat of the glacier ice and accumulation of meltwater in the depression remaining. The rocky debris pile of a terminal moraine shows the one-time extent of the ice. The Challenger Glacier may continue to shrink, like most of the glaciers in the North Cascades in recent years, or, given a return of cooler weather, may once again begin to grow.

JOHN DITTLI

where the rate of melting or *ablation* is greater than the rate of accumulation.

The movement of a glacier is its most characteristic feature and distinguishes glaciers from permanent but nonmoving snowfields. Deep cracks in the ice, called *crevasses* (cre·VAS·es), are evidence of this movement. A moving glacier also causes erosion, created by the abrasive scouring action of rock fragments that fall from valley walls and are incorporated into the ice. This erosion contributes to several of the most distinguishing glacial landforms: cirques, arêtes, horns, tarns, troughs, hanging valleys, and moraines.

At the upper ends of alpine glaciers, at the head of the accumulation zone, lie steep-walled semicircular basins known as *cirques*. Cirque basins are characterized by steep, rocky headwalls resulting from the glacier's having carved into the rocks above. Meltwater, trickling into small cracks in the rocks, freezes and expands, shattering the rock, as does the constant cycle of freeze-thaw action. Cirque bottoms often contain lovely small lakes called *tarns*—remnants of the scouring action of ice and melting snow. The joys of camping or bivouacking at a remote tarn are one of the pleasures of wilderness mountaineering in the North Cascades.

A deep crevasse, called a *bergschrund*, forms at the head of a glacier where the ice pulls away from the adjacent snow and rock. Bergshrunds can be forbidding obstacles to climbers, and crossing or getting around a 'schrund is often the most difficult part of climbing the mountain.

As cirques on opposite sides of a ridge grow, cutting deeper and deeper into the divide, a sharp, narrow, serrated ridge called an *arête* (ah·RET) is formed. The North Cascades are known for their extensive alpine glaciation, and the many high cirque basins connected by sheer and twisted arêtes bear witness to the mighty rivers of ice that carved them. The Picket Range, in the northern section of the park, consists of many narrow, nearly vertical arêtes connecting cirque basins, of which the ridges between Luna and MacMillan cirques are the largest and most spectacular. When cirques on two sides of a ridge break through and meet, the resulting low point, known as a *col* (KOL), or, if larger, a pass, may provide an inviting route for adventurous mountaineers. Cache Col provides just such a route for climbers traversing south from Cascade Pass towards Mount Formidable and Glacier Peak.

The spirelike pyramidal summit of Mount Shuksan is a classic example of a *horn*—a peak formed by three or more cirques that have cut

Glacial Effects
Common to North Cascades National Park

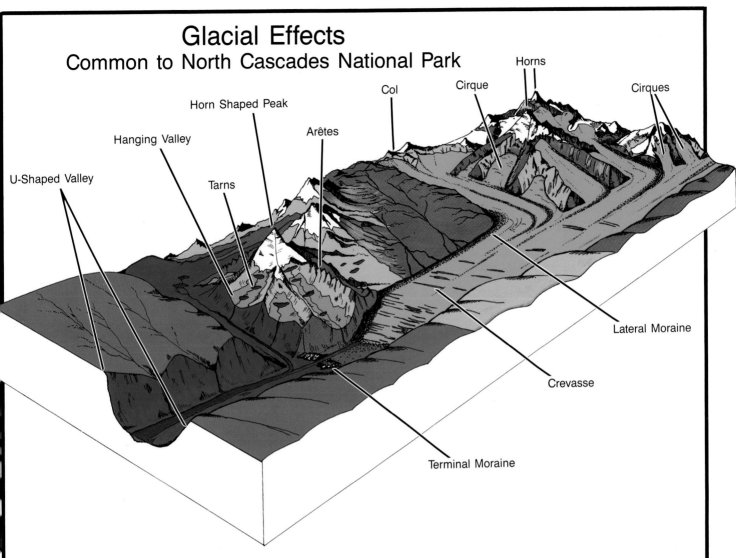

Mountain glaciers, formed by perpetual snow, vastly change the topography as they flow relentlessly downhill in a river of ice. The illustration above demonstrates the effect of glaciers retreating across typical North Cascade terrain. Glacier ice erodes and chisels the landscape gouging out bowl-shaped ampitheaters called "cirques." Two cirques that meet are separated by an "arête" — a sharp ridge resembling a fish bone. The meeting of three cirques forms a "horn-shaped peak," and where cirques break through each other, a saddle-like "col" forms. Lakes created in cirques are called "tarns." Where streams once had rounded ridges and gentle slopes in V-shaped valleys, the glacial ice moving through leaves a "U-shaped" profile.

The propulsive flow of glacial ice moves in varying ways in different parts of the glacier. The "firn line" noted in the illustration shows the gradual change between the zone of accumulation and the zone of wastage.

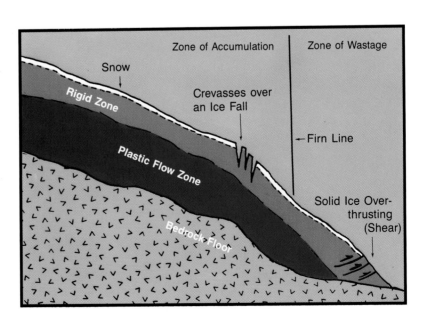

The sheer northwest face of Luna Peak, easternmost outlying peak of the northern Picket Range, plunges 4,500 feet into the valleys of Luna and Big Beaver creeks. Fresh snow clings to the ledges and cracks of the fractured rock. The long gentle southwest ridge is most often climbed by mountaineers, the fractured rock of the northeast face has not yet been climbed.

BOB & IRA SPRING

SAUL WEISBERG

The sheer north faces of the southern Pickets form the headwall of McMillan Cirque. Scoured by ice and storms and carved by glaciers plucking at their flanks, these peaks provide a formidable challenge for mountaineers. From left: McMillan Spires, Inspiration Peak, Mount Degenhardt, Mount Terror, and The Rake.

back into the mountain mass. On Mount Shuksan, the Price, Sulphide, Curtis, and Crystal glaciers have all carved deeply into the mountain, forming the beautiful peak we see today.

As glaciers move they scrape and grind away the underlying rock. The debris that results from the erosion is eventually deposited along the front and sides of the moving ice as *moraines*. Moraines appear as heaped-up piles of unsorted rock. A *terminal* moraine is formed at the terminus of the glacier as the melting ice drops the rock debris it has been carrying. A *lateral* moraine forms along the sides of the glacier. As opposed to landforms created by the scouring, erosive powers of glaciers, moraines are depositional landforms. Another depositional landform, glacial erratics, are large boulders that were carried by moving ice, then dropped when the glacier began its retreat.

Modern glaciers are only remnants of the ice that once covered the North Cascades. In ages past, glaciers were more extensive and reached much lower elevations than they do today. Evidence for prior glaciation includes large U-shaped valleys, semicircular cirque basins, glacial striations and erratics, moraines, arêtes, horns, and tarns. Glaciers advance and retreat in response to changing climatic conditions. There are presently over 300 active glaciers within North Cascades National Park—and as many more in the rest of the range.

Why do mountains of only moderate height carry so much ice and snow? The answer is the essence of the North Cascades: water. Running parallel to the coast and only 30 miles from Puget Sound, the North Cascades intercept the storms that sweep in from the Pacific. As the warm, moisture-laden air is pushed up against the mountains it rises, cools, and drops its moisture as rain and snow. Average annual precipitation on the west side of the range is 110 inches. The winter season may deposit as much as 46 feet of snow. Snow often falls in September and lasts through early July. The accumulation of snow and frequent storms in the spring and fall combine with generally cool temperatures to promote the conditions necessary for the formation and maintenance of glaciers.

JOHN DITTLI

The Green Lake Glacier on Bacon Peak shows a regular pattern of crevasses, perpendicular to the direction of movement of the flowing ice.

BECKY & GARY VESTAL

The classic U-shaped valley of the North Fork of the Cascade River shows clearly that glacial ice once filled this canyon. Trees manage to retain a foothold in areas swept clean by winter avalanches. The ice-cream cone summit of Eldorado Peak is visible in the distance.

NPS PHOTO

Fjord-like, Ross Lake twists 22 miles to the Canadian border. Downstream its waters generate one-third of Seattle's electricity.

The east side of the North Cascades lies in a rain shadow formed by the Cascade Crest. Precipitation on the east side averages 35 inches yearly at Lake Chelan (sha·LAN) and only 12 inches in the nearby Pasayten (pa·SAY·ten) Wilderness. Obviously the west side is where the majority of active glaciers remain.

Within the past two to three million years, a cool, wet climate created large alpine glaciers that flowed down the valleys from the high peaks. Episodes of alpine glaciation occurred repeatedly, most recently about 20,000 years ago. Ice covered all but the highest peaks. The present landscape of the North Cascades was carved during this

time. The North Cascades Highway follows glacial troughs along the U-shaped valley of the Skagit River. Lake Chelan is another spectacular example of a glacial trough. It was excavated to a depth of over 2,000 feet by a glacier that once flowed down the Stehekin River valley from Cascade Pass.

Mount Baker and Glacier Peak, two 10,000-foot volcanoes, are covered with extensive glaciers, as are all the higher, nonvolcanic peaks such as Mount Shuksan, Mount Buckner, Mount Challenger, and Eldorado Peak. These older, nonvolcanic peaks show the effects of glacial activity and erosion more than the younger volcanoes.

As alpine glaciers flow downslope they follow the path of least resistance—through valleys. The erosive power of the ice carves wide U-shaped valleys known as glacial troughs. Valleys along Goodell Creek and the Cascade River have flat bottoms and steep sides resulting from the glaciers that once carved them. Smaller side-valleys containing alpine glaciers were often left "hanging" when the ice receded. Pelton Basin, just east of Cascade pass, is an excellent example of a hanging valley, dropping off abruptly into the valley of the Stehekin River.

Nearly all the large river valleys of the North Cascades were carved by alpine glaciers at one time or another. The valleys of the Nooksack and Stehekin rivers played host to large rivers of ice in the last two to three million years. The Stehekin Valley and Lake Chelan are classic examples of glacial basins.

The Skagit River valley between Newhalem (new·HALE·em) and Ross Dam is an interesting exception to the general trend. Downstream from Newhalem, glacial erosion is present as the result of the large continental ice sheet that moved upvalley from Puget Sound. North of Ross Dam the Skagit Valley was carved by another lobe of the glacier that moved south from British Columbia. Between these two points the Skagit River flows through an unglaciated V-shaped valley caused by stream erosion.

Most streams in the North Cascades have glacial origins, arising as meltwater from the mighty rivers of ice. These glacial streams carry high levels of crushed and powdered rock particles, called glacial flour, that give the water a distinctive ap-

JOHN DITTLI

Even in summer, ice floats on the green glacial waters of a tarn below the icefall of the terminus of the Bacon Peak Glacier.

Sun-bleached snags of whitebark pine frame Lake Ann, a small lake nestled below Maple Pass. To the east rise the jagged crags of Liberty Bell Mountain and Early Winter Spires. The scarcity of glaciers, vegetation adapted to more arid conditions, and dry open slopes all point to a relative lack of precipitation on the east side of the range.

pearance. Diablo Lake reflects a dark green color from suspended mineral sediments. Higher in the mountains many streams appear cloudy because of the sediment load. Streams, unlike glaciers, cut narrow V-shaped valleys as they erode into the surface of the land. By looking at its profile it is generally possible to detect whether a valley was glaciated in the past, although most glacial valleys now have streams running through them that continue the erosion begun by glacial ice and ancient streams.

SUGGESTED READING

ALT, DAVID, and DONALD W. HYNDAM. *Northwest Exposures: A Geologic Story of the Northwest.* Missoula, Montana: Mountain Press Publishing Company, 1995.

HARRIS, ANN G., and ESTHER TUTTLE. Chapter 26: "North Cascades National Park." In *Geology of National Parks.* 4th ed. Dubuque, Iowa: Kendall/Hunt Publications, 1983.

MCKEE, BATES. *Cascadia: The Geologic Evolution of the Pacific Northwest.* New York: McGraw-Hill Book Company, 1972.

The Living Mountains

In the first light of morning the clear, flutelike song of a hermit thrush drifts through a mountain meadow. A marmot's shrill whistle, piercing the sky, warns of a golden eagle soaring high above the ridge crest. Mist rises slowly from the valley below as the rhythmic drumming of a male blue grouse welcomes the new day. In this land of abundant rainfall and early snows, of high peaks and deep valleys, the sounds of life are everywhere.

The mountain world of the North Cascades is a rich and varied ecosystem—a place bound together by geography and climate and by the interactions of living communities of plants and animals. It is the dramatic changes that we notice first: the sharp contrast between old-growth forests of the river valleys and dwarfed and twisted

This great blue heron hunts for fish and amphibians in the still waters of a lowland pool.

JOHN DITTLI

PAT O'HARA

krummholz trees of an alpine ridge; the difference between lush greenery of the west side and drier forests of the eastern slope. Not all the differences between habitats are dramatic, however. There are many subtle changes to notice as one habitat and community grade almost imperceptibly into another.

Within the North Cascades ecosystem there are many different habitats. These range from the microhabitat of the forest floor—a world of fir needles and decaying wood that is home to the banana slug and wolf spider—to the trout-filled waters of Berdeen Lake, hidden away in the backcountry and accessible only by two days of rugged cross-country travel. The mountain forests support communities of plants and animals different from those of the river valleys; plants that flourish in subalpine meadows are strangers to the more severe conditions occuring on alpine

Two subspecies of deer are found in the North Cascades: the blacktail deer (shown here), common on the west side of the range, and the mule deer, found on the east side. Interbreeding occurs along the Cascade Crest.

ridges. Ecologists compare an organism's habitat to its "address." This habitat is a combination of the physical environment, the rocks and land and water, as well as all the other organisms that live in the same place. Together these plants and animals make up an interacting, interdependent community.

As we hike up the river valley toward the montane forest the plants and animals change around us. Giant red cedars of the lowlands give way to Douglas fir and Pacific silver fir. Merganser and harlequin ducks of the lower river make way for dippers and spotted sandpipers. As we leave the river behind and climb higher we enter the subalpine world of meadows and stunted krummholz trees. At the pass, gateway to the peaks beyond, we find ourselves in a different land filled with different creatures—a world apart

from the valley still shrouded in mist far, far below.

In these high meadows the dominant life forms are small cushion plants; low-growing, prostrate masses of green with bright-colored flowers. Climbing higher, toward the glacial snows, we enter a world of rock and ice. Along the rocky summit ridge of the peak the only living things we find are lichens, a few insects, and two rosy finches, squeaking as they hop on the topmost crags, oblivious to the precipice below.

There are few untrammeled wilderness areas left in the world; North Cascades National Park is one of them. Its many habitats and natural communities have been preserved in as pristine a

JOHN DITTLI

lake nestled beneath the rock towers of Mount Spickard.

Over millions of years of geologic time, living things have become superbly adapted to their environment. Through the process of evolution every species has become uniquely fitted to its habitat and community. Life is limited by the physical environment (temperature, wind, moisture, space, length of growing season) and by other organisms (competition and predation). An organism must be able to cope with all of these to survive.

RIVER VALLEYS, LAKES, AND MONTANE FORESTS

Water: cascading water, flowing water, still water. Water is the essence of the North Cascades. Small creeks and rivulets tumble from glaciers and snowfields and join together as rushing creeks—creeks that would be called rivers anywhere else. These tributary streams finally merge into the mighty rivers of the western slope: Chilliwack, Baker, Skagit, and Nooksack. On the east side of the range there is less rainfall and therefore fewer glaciers. The Stehekin River drains the southeast corner of North Cascades National Park, while the watersheds of the Methow and Pasayten rivers drain the eastern slopes of the Pasayten Wilderness east of Ross Lake.

There are hundreds of small lakes scattered throughout the North Cascades. Most of these lakes are isolated jewels of the mountains, accessible only by arduous cross-country hiking. These tarns, remnants of the alpine glaciers that once covered the North Cascades, are rich reservoirs of life surrounded by marshes and meadows. Voracious dragonfly nymphs are common in streams and lakes, as are caddisfly and mayfly larvae. Rainbow and cutthroat trout have been introduced into many of the high lakes, where they feed upon abundant aquatic insects.

The larger lakes, including Ross Lake and Lake Chelan, host breeding populations of common loons and other fish-eating birds. Common mergansers, large diving ducks, are frequently seen along rivers, as are great blue herons and spotted

state as possible. These communities exist now as they have existed for thousands of years. They are living preserves where we can experience the natural world as it existed before the arrival of industrialized civilization.

Many organisms and communities can exist only in a truly wild state. The introduction of the human presence drives away many species, the grizzly and the wolf included, in search of undisturbed terrain. Several locations within North Cascades National Park have been set aside as research natural areas—special places designated as reserves for studying the ecology of natural communities. These include Boston Glacier, containing the largest glacier in the park; Pyramid Lake, containing an endangered population of rough-skinned newts; and Silver Lake, an alpine

Canoeists explore one of the many inlets along Ross Lake. Easy access to the lake is available only from the north, via Canada and Hozomeen campground. From the south, canoeists portage around Ross Dam or carry their boats down a short trail from the highway. This helps preserve the wilderness quality of Ross Lake.

KEITH GUNNAR

sandpipers. Ospreys fish the rivers and lakes; they dive from hundreds of feet above the water, then rise with struggling trout clutched tightly in their talons.

Hiking trails wind through most of the major river valleys. Travel off-trail is difficult at best and nearly impossible in many places; river valleys are impenetrable jungles of vegetation. Creeks and stream-bank habitats are choked with armies of inhospitable brush including spiny devil's club, prickly currant, salmonberry, thimbleberry, and willows. There are tales of mountaineers who spent days trying to bushwack cross-country out from the Picket Range—crawling through brush that yielded less than a mile's passage for each day's effort.

Let us instead hike up a trail along Big Beaver Creek as it winds its way into the heart of the North Cascades wilderness. The greatest concentration of old-growth red cedar in the North Cascades is found along the lower reaches of Big Beaver Creek below 2,000 feet altitude. These magnificent trees are the guardians of the lower valley.

A hiker breaks into the open through a green wall of bracken fern while bushwhacking in Big Beaver Valley. The vegetation in the lower valleys grows fast—trail crews must open trails each year to maintain passage.

JOHN DITTLI

Water is the essence of the North Cascades. From the snows of the Challenger Glacier thousands of waterfalls cascade into Little Beaver Canyon. These glacial-carved valleys are covered with lush vegetation as plants scramble for a toehold on the steep slopes. A moderate, marine-influenced climate brings frequent rain, and with it the cascades that gave these mountains their name.

Red cedars grow in moist habitats. Thus they are ideally suited to the North Cascades, where summers are cloudy and winters are mild. Tapering from heavily buttressed bases 10 feet in diameter, they rise 200 feet above the forest floor balanced on a shallow, wide-spreading root system that provides stability in the wet valley soils. They are distinguished by their stringy, fibrous bark, which peels away in thin strips. Lacy sprays of flat needles make up the foliage, giving red cedars a delicate appearance despite their great size. Red cedars are a long-lived species; the oldest are estimated to be over 1,000 years old. Native peoples of the Pacific Northwest used all parts of the cedar— the bark for clothing and the wood for totems, dugouts, and lodging.

The other dominant tree of the river valleys is western hemlock. Both western red cedar and western hemlock are shade tolerant; their seedlings thrive in the dense shade of lowland forests. Together these two trees dominate the *climax* com-

munity of the low-elevation forests of the North Cascades. (*Climax* is the endpoint in a ecological process known as *succession,* whereby one community replaces another over time in response to changing environmental conditions.) Growing in scattered open glades throughout this cedar-hemlock forest are red alder and bigleaf maple. These two deciduous trees must have at least some scattered sunlight for their seedlings to grow. They make their appearance along trails and streams and in openings created when one of the forest giants falls during a winter windstorm. Red alder is an important pioneer species that adds nitrogen to the soil through nodules of symbiotic bacteria on its roots. With its giant five-lobed leaves spanning 16 inches or more, bigleaf maple is easy to identify.

As we walk along the forest trail, occasionally climbing over fallen trees and ducking under low-hanging branches, we see a spectrum of all the many shades of green. Huckleberries tantalize the hiker along the trail. In drier locations salal (sal·LAL) and Oregon grape, both evergreen shrubs, dominate the understory, while sword-fern and its many relatives grow throughout the forest. In springtime the forest floor is thick with wildflowers. Trillium, bleedingheart, yellow violet, calpyso orchid, twinflower, and bunchberry display their delicate colors and brighten the forest shade. Mosses, lichens, and fungi grow thickly over the ground and on exposed rock and fallen trees.

As our trail ascends we leave the river valley and enter the mountain forest of Beaver Pass. There is no clear dividing line between these two habitats, just a gradual change in the physical environment, and with it, a corresponding change

BECKY & GARY VESTAL

The first snow of the season finds the red leaves of this vine maple still clinging to their branch.

in the plant and animal communities. We begin to feel a slight chill in the air, bringing an awareness of the snowy peaks that rise from these mountain forests. As we climb, the land becomes drier and more open. The red cedars are left behind, and a mixture of western hemlock and Pacific silver fir dominate the forest. Red alder, Douglas fir, and bigleaf maple still grow in sunlit openings.

Every now and then our trail crosses an open slope—the remnants of avalanches that thunder down from the surrounding peaks every winter. These avalanche paths are choked with brush. Vine maple and many other shrubs compete vigorously for space and light. At about 4,500 feet elevation western hemlock is replaced by mountain hemlock in the forest canopy, and we find ourselves hiking through a silver fir–mountain

BOB & IRA SPRING

Western red cedars and vine maples shade a thick ground cover of thimbleberry and false Solomon's seal along a secluded forest trail in the Big Beaver Valley.

Overleaf: The west face of Mount Shuksan rises above Picture Lake and Heather Meadows. Photo by Jeff Gnass.

The north-facing ramparts of Mount Redoubt tower above a sparse forest of subalpine firs. The tall, spire-like shape of the firs is an adaptation to shedding heavy snowfall. The flat valley bottom is wet much of the year as shown by the profusion of moisture-loving willows.

Tolmie's saxifrage, an alpine species, forms a garden in the rocks above timberline. The root of the word "saxifrage" means "rock breaker."

hemlock forest as we continue our climb toward timberline.

On the drier east side of the North Cascades a similar change is taking place, although different trees are involved. Douglas fir and ponderosa pine grow at lower elevations. At higher altitudes they are replaced by western larch, lodgepole pine, and Englemann spruce. Western hemlock and red cedar are not as common. Black cottonwoods and willows line the rivers. With open landscapes and a relative absence of brush, the east side of the North Cascades invites the cross-country explorer.

The Subalpine and Alpine Worlds

As our trail winds higher into the mountains we round a corner where the dense stands of silver fir and mountain hemlock give way to open meadows and windblown ridges. We have entered the subalpine, gateway to the land above the trees. The subalpine world is characterized by the absence of continuous forest. It is a land of lush wildflower meadows, scattered groves of dwarf trees, and a varied group of plant and animal communities distinct from the forests below. On the western side of the North Cascades the subalpine zone begins at 5,500 feet. Less snow accumulation and a longer growing season on the eastern slope push the lower limit of the subalpine up to 6,500 feet.

The elevation at which timberline occurs is determined by a combination of factors, including temperature, snow, and wind. Snowpack affects the length of the growing season and the amount of soil moisture available throughout the year, and both of these affect the ability of trees to survive. The common timberline trees of the western slope of the North Cascades are mountain hemlock and subalpine fir, although Pacific silver fir and Alaska yellow-cedar are also found at its lower levels. On the eastern slope subalpine fir, Engelmann spruce, subalpine larch, and whitebark pine comprise the highest stands of trees.

As we climb higher we notice that the shapes of the trees change radically—from large and upright to stunted dwarf *krummholz* forms, often growing in small clumps or tree islands. Krummholz is a German word meaning "crooked wood," which graphically describes the gnarled and twisted forms that trees take at timberline. These tree islands usually become established around a single tree whose presence modifies the environment in its immediate vicinity. Its darker color causes earlier snowmelt and provides protection from the wind, allowing seedlings to become well established.

Subalpine trees commonly reproduce by layering; a branch touches the ground, takes root, and eventually becomes an independent tree. This leads to the common pattern of krummholz islands, with an upright tree in the center of a dense "skirt" of limbs and new shoots spreading around it. The height of the skirt is regulated by the depth of winter snow—branches that protrude above the protective snowpack are pruned back by wind and blowing ice.

The transition from mountain forest to subalpine meadow is dramatic. Trees disappear, replaced by grasses, herbaceous flowers, and small shrubs. Lush meadows of alpine phlox, Davidson's penstemon, false hellebore, Sitka valerian, mountain lupine, partridge foot, fanleaf cinquefoil, and glacier lily cover the slopes with a riotous display of color. Patterns of snow accumulation

Perennial glacier lilies are among the first flowers to bloom in the spring, often bursting into color before the snow is gone. Covering the subalpine meadows in June and early July, they have set seed and disappeared by August.

Sunlight illuminates the bark of the aptly named Pacific silver fir, dominant tree of mid-elevation montane forests. A diminutive foam flower, another member of the saxifrage family, nestles at its base.

JOHN DITTLI

JOHN DITTLI

and snowmelt are the determining factors in the distribution of subalpine plant communities. Snow blown off the higher alpine ridges accumulates on leeward slopes, where luxuriant subalpine meadows thrive on meltwater in early summer.

In wetter subalpine habitats red and yellow monkeyflower, bog orchid, marsh marigold, purple gentian, and many species of saxifrage provide a brilliant display. Subalpine vegetation may be covered with snow well into July in many places. Dwarf sedge dominates these snowbank communities. In the western North Cascades the growing season usually lasts less than three months before winter storms begin again.

Contrasting with the dense herbaceous growth of the subalpine, the alpine zone is a more severe and limited habitat. The alpine *tundra*, from a Russian word meaning "treeless plain," is a harsh world dominated by the interaction of wind and snow. Storms and freezing weather can occur in any month of the year. Temperatures range from below freezing to over 90° Fahrenheit in August. Lichens, mosses, and prostrate cushion plants are the dominant life forms.

Water is a severely limiting element in the alpine environment. Exposed ridges are blown free of winter snow. Rocky, nutrient-poor soils retain little moisture for plant growth. Strong, desiccating winds help remove what water remains. These factors combine to cause a summer drought in the high alpine country of the North Cascades. Frost action and soil movement make it difficult for plants to take root and survive. Sheltered microhabitats promote the accumulation of moisture and the establishment of seedlings. Amidst the rocks, cushion plants like alpine phlox, moss campion, and Tolmie's saxifrage grow in sheltered crevices.

The seeds of this western anemone are dispersed across the mountain world by the wind.

BOB & IRA SPRING

Sky pilot, an alpine polemonium, grows from a narrow crack in the rocks high above timberline.

Many insects specialize in pollinating particular flowers. This syrphid fly is pollinating a columbine.

BECKY & GARY VESTAL

Adaptations of Alpine Plants and Animals

Alpine plants rely on many specialized adaptations in order to survive in a severe environment characterized by cold temperatures, a short growing season, and poor, unstable soil. The majority of alpine plants are characterized by a low, prostrate growth form that hugs the warmer and less windy microclimate near the ground. Most alpine plants are perennials, for dependence upon annual seed production is not adaptive in the alpine environment. Dwarf sedge, glacier lily, and false hellebore even begin growing beneath the snow.

Root systems in alpine plants are well developed, providing food storage as well as an efficient means of obtaining nutrients from poor soil. In response to moisture stress many alpine plants may be covered with silky hairs or form thick, waxy leaves to prevent water loss. Small woody shrubs such as the red, yellow, and white heathers

Monkshood grows in moist places in forests and subalpine meadows.

What happened here? Yellow monkey flower, a common subalpine plant of wet meadows, grows next to the leg bone of a mountain goat.

Red Indian paintbrush depends upon soil bacteria and other plant associations to live.

Pink mountain heather is a fragile woody plant of the high meadows.

JOHN DITTLI

The hoary marmot is a common resident of subalpine meadows and rockslides. Marmots live in colonies consisting of several adults and up to a dozen of their immature offspring. Often seen lazing in the sun on boulders, they are quick to sound their high-pitched warning whistle and retreat into their burrows when danger threatens.

are evergreen; by retaining their leaves throughout the winter they are ready to begin growing as soon as spring arrives.

Magnificent large blossoms of many subalpine flowers are an adaptation for pollination. Insect pollinators are hampered by low temperatures and overcast days that are common in the alpine zone. Large flowers serve as an excellent means of attracting the insects necessary to pollinate a plant. Wildflowers such as the pealike lupine even have a built-in means of indicating when pollination has occurred. The blossoms change color from blue to purple after they have been visited by an insect.

The major difference between plant and animal adaptations to life in the North Cascades is a basic one: animals can move. Humans are most commonly found in the high mountains during summer, and most of the animals we see at that time are also summer residents. During especially fierce storms many alpine birds and mammals temporarily leave the high country for more protected regions below. Migration to or from the high mountains can occur on a seasonal or a daily basis. Deer often enter the subalpine meadows to browse, but rarely stray far from the protection of the forest. Most alpine animals use microhabitats extensively, especially small rock crevices and the shelter provided by krummholz clumps. In the winter most true alpine mammals hibernate in burrows below the ground.

Low temperatures by themselves are not a limiting factor for alpine animals. The short growing season in the alpine, coupled with a lack of food, high winds, and extreme environmental diversity, are the major stresses to be dealt with.

Birds are the most mobile animals, and many commute daily to the land above the trees from roosting sites in the montane forests below. The reverse is done by the black swifts that nest in small crevices in high cliffs; they fly many miles into the lowlands to catch insects that they take back to their young. During long storms the metabolism of the young birds slows down, enabling them to survive for extensive periods without food. Ravens are one of the most characteristic of mountain birds; their black visage and hoarse croaking can be heard at all elevations.

Distribution of birds changes with habitat and elevation. The buzzing song of the varied thrush can be heard in valley forests. In lowland mead-

BECKY & GARY VESTAL

Adapted to survive in the most rugged of mountains, the mountain goat's thick white coat repels winter storms while its flexible toes conform to the smallest ledges. In winter, goats seek out windswept ridges to feed, or descend to lower elevations. Young are born in early June, often on the most remote crags.

Black bears, weighing from 200 to more than 400 pounds, are common throughout the North Cascades. Often occurring in brown and cinnamon as well as black, they are more active at night than during the day. Grizzly bears were probably once numerous, but were hunted extensively. They survive in very small numbers in the North Cascades.

ows it is replaced by the musical tones of Swainson's thrush, whereas the flutelike song of the hermit thrush predominates in higher subalpine meadows.

Other birds spend most of their time in the alpine world. Rosy finches are small, gray, sparrowlike birds commonly found on the highest summits. They feed on seeds and small insects that are blown onto the snow. Horned larks and water pipits are two small songbirds that commonly inhabit subalpine meadows and alpine ridges. Both spend most of their time on the ground, searching for insects to carry to the young in their carefully concealed ground nests. These three species are among the few that actually breed above timberline—although they retreat to warmer regions in the winter. Many birds undertake a vertical migration, dropping to lower elevations for the winter instead of migrating south.

The white-tailed ptarmigan, a member of the grouse family, is covered with pure white feathers in the winter for camouflage against the snow. It also has a thick covering of feathers on its feet, allowing it to walk on top of the snow. As the snow melts in the spring the ptarmigan gradually replaces its white feathers with brown plumage that conceals it from predators for the rest of the

During the winter mule deer descend to the lowlands where food is more abundant. In spring they move upward with the melting snow. Here a doe browses in a meadow of lupine, sitka valerian, and false hellebore.

The western tanager is a common migrant and summer resident of open forests and mountain slopes. In late summer and fall they may appear anywhere throughout the mountains. The brilliantly colored male is one of our most beautiful birds.

NPS PHOTO BY R. J. HENTGES

year. Often called "fool's hen" by the early miners, the ptarmigan is relatively unwary and permits humans to make a close approach.

Marmots and pikas are two of the most easily seen, and heard, alpine mammals. From Whatcom (WAT·come) Pass large hoary marmots, relatives of the woodchuck, can be seen sprawled out, sleeping in the sun on broad, flat boulders. They may appear lazy, but they are constantly on the lookout for danger. An approaching coyote or eagle—or backpacker—results in a loud, piercing whistle that alerts all members of the colony that an intruder is near. The pika, or cony, is a small relative of the rabbit, but with shorter ears. Its high-pitched, nasal squeak gives it away as it scurries from rock to rock, carrying bunches of leaves and grasses to store in piles underground.

The pika does not hibernate during the winter but remains active, running back and forth to its "hay piles" until released from its subterranean life by the melting snow.

The highest and most remote ridges are home to mountain goats. In summer these uncommon residents of the high crags live well above timberline, retreating to the forest edges only when forced downward by severe winter storms. These skilled mountaineers of the animal world tread easily across the precipitous rock faces of the most rugged peaks.

Even icy glaciers are not devoid of life. Threadlike ice worms live within the surface layers of frozen glacier ice. Carnivorous invertebrates, including several spiders, compete with rosy finches in stalking windblown insects on the ice.

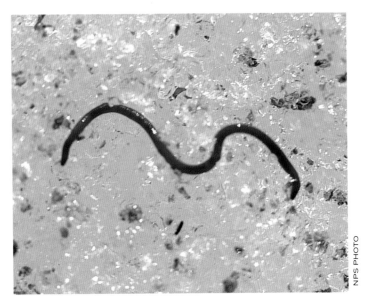

NPS PHOTO

Adapted to living inside a glacier—these minute iceworms spend their entire lives within a sea of ice. Related to the common earthworm, half-inch-long iceworms are found in temperate-climate glaciers only, where water exists in equilibrium with ice. Unable to tolerate freezing, the worms migrate vertically through the top several feet of ice, swimming through the ice water surrounding the ice crystals. In the late afternoon they come to the surface to feed on pollen and algae blown onto the surface. Sometimes occurring in densities greater than 500 per square meter, iceworms are thought to have evolved from aquatic worms that moved into the ice from glacial-fed streams.

The raven, often seen soaring high over the peaks, is a year-round resident of the mountain landscape.

NPS PHOTO BY J. R. DOUGLAS

The white-tailed ptarmigan needs both summer and winter camouflage for life in the alpine world.

JOHN DITTLI

This western tiger swallowtail is one of the most common butterflies of the lowlands on both sides of the mountains. There are many other similar "swallow-tailed" butterflies.

Amidst the larger wildlife of the North Cascades there flies a smaller and more subtle beauty. Small bits of color flutter through the meadows—the butterflies of the mountain world. Butterflies are common in flowered meadows and forest glades but are only visible when the twin conditions of warmth and sunlight are present. A large, bright yellow butterfly with black longitudinal "tiger stripes" and a prominent tail on each hind wing, the western tiger swallowtail is one of the most beautiful butterflies of the Pacific Northwest. Other gaudy species of the lowlands include Lorquin's admiral and the painted lady.

It is in the higher subalpine meadows that the butterflies really come into their own. Common butterflies of higher elevations include the blues, coppers, hairstreaks, and fritillaries. A distinctive group of the highest elevations are the arctics and alpines—small, dark-colored wisps of the wind. The arctics and the alpines belong to a family known as the Satyrs, named after the denizens of mythology. These inconspicuous creatures of the alpine landscape reward the careful observer with their delicate beauty.

SUGGESTED READING

ARNO, STEPHEN F., and RAMONA P. HAMMERLY. *Northwest Trees*. Seattle, Washington: The Mountaineers, 1977.

MATHEWS, DANIEL. *Cascade-Olympic Natural History*. Portland, Oregon: Raven Editions, 1992.

POJAR, JIM, and ANDY MACKINNON. *Plants of the Pacific Northwest Coast*. Vancouver, British Columbia: Lone Pine Publishing, 1994.

TAYLOR, RONALD J., and GEORGE W. DOUGLAS. *Mountain Plants of the Pacific Northwest*. Seattle, Washington: The Mountaineers, 1995.

The "Lady of the Lake" makes a daily round trip
on Lake Chelan to the remote community of Stehekin.

MIKE BARNHART

Lake Chelan
National Recreation Area

Lake Chelan NRA is administered as one of the three units of North Cascades National Park Service Complex. Boating, fishing, hiking, horseback riding, and cross-country skiing are among the area's main attractions. Lake Chelan is the third deepest lake in the United States, with a maximum depth of 1,500 feet. At the head of the 55-mile-long lake lies the Stehekin Valley, stretching 25 miles into the mountains to the headwaters of the Stehekin River at Cascade Pass. The Indian word "stehekin" means "the way through," and early native Americans traveled regularly over Cascade Pass on their way back and forth over the mountains. The National Park Service maintains a small visitor center at Stehekin, and the local community provides abundant recreational opportunities. Access is by boat, plane, packsaddle, or foot only.

NANCY BARNHART

Arriving by float plane provides another option for traveling to and from Stehekin. The scenery is no less spectacular, and the ride is quicker, but for some people the rapid means of transportation seems to shrink the boundaries of wilderness.

34

KEITH GUNNAR

Trail riders leave from Stehekin as autumn colors begin
to paint the high country. Horseback riding is popular
in the dry open country of the east side of the range.

KEITH GUNNAR

Visitors aboard the "Lady of the Lake" pause to
watch mountain goats feeding along a precipitous
cliff along Lake Chelan. It was to preserve a
dwindling population of mountain goats that one
of the first calls went out for the establishment
of a national park here as early as 1892.

Cottonwood and alder leaves
cover the ground as cold nights and short days
bring summer to a close.

35

In the lower Stehekin Valley, Rainbow Falls becomes an icicle-draped spectacle in winter. During the summer shuttle buses provide easy access to the falls. In winter skis may be the only way in.

MIKE BARNHART

DIANE ALLEN

Big-leaf maple is one of the first trees to bloom in the Stehekin Valley.

K. C. DEN DOOVEN

JOHN DITTLI

An old farm truck waits out the end of its days as spare parts hang in the workshop of the Buckner Homestead.
The William Buckner family began a 59-year history of living and farming in the valley when they purchased 147 acres from William Buzzard, one of the first settlers, in 1911.
They planted an apple orchard which continues to produce.
Out-buildings, including a shop, barn, and cabin, were added over the years. In 1970 the National Park Service purchased most of the original homestead.

MIKE BARNHART

The Stehekin River rises dramatically every spring as melting snow in the mountains floods the lower valleys. The river's power often washes out part of the road between Stehekin and Cottonwood.

JOHN DITTLI

DIANE ALLEN

A hiker walks through fall color on the trail to Cascade Pass as vine maples begin to turn in September.

Those Who Came Before . . .

Indians of the North Cascades were hunters, fishers, and gatherers who lived in a severe and changing environment. Their life was closely tied to the natural environment and was vulnerable to changes in the abundance or scarcity of the resources they depended upon.

To understand prehistoric use of the North Cascades by native peoples we must realize that for them this land was not a wilderness. They had lived for thousands of generations in the mountain environment. They were intimately acquainted with the land, the trees, plants and animals, rivers and peaks, all of which had names and meaning. The mountain world was their home—supplying their needs for food and shelter and providing a base for their culture. Native American interactions with the environment were flexible and adaptable to rapidly changing conditions. They made use of all altitudinal zones, using different areas of the mountains for different purposes at different seasons as food-gathering and settlement needs required.

The rugged topography of the North Cascades separates two regions that contained large native populations: the peoples of the Pacific Northwest/Puget Lowlands to the west and those of the Columbia River Basin to the east. These Native Americans were connected by a trade network that enabled them to share locally abundant resources for materials they lacked. All travelers in the North Cascades must of necessity follow the path of least resistance. The extreme topography places practical limitations on where humans can go, thus an intimate knowledge of the land is necessary. Like modern climbers and backpackers, prehistoric Indians followed ridge crests whenever possible to avoid the dense, tangled brush of the river bottoms.

The oldest artifacts found in North Cascades National Park are projectile points from a site near Hozomeen (HO·zo·meen), at the north end of what is now Ross Lake. Preliminary dating of these points indicates that this site was occupied, either continuously or intermittently, for over 8,000 years. It is uncertain whether the Indians who lived here were ancestors of the five Indian tribes living within North Cascades National Park at the time of initial contact with white explorers in 1800.

These five Salishan-speaking tribes were the *Nooksack*, living along the Nooksack River; the *Chilliwack*, along the lower Chilliwack River and Chilliwack Lake; the *Chelan*, along the Stehekin

NPS PHOTO

Who was the artist? These prehistoric pictographs were painted on a rock wall along Lake Chelan long before the earliest white explorers arrived in the area. They demonstrate that the original inhabitants of the land pursued a rich cultural, spiritual and artistic tradition.

Humans have approached the mountain in many ways and for many reasons—for necessities for adventure, and for inspiration

The jagged peaks of Silver Star Mountain show the magic and mystery of the North Cascades. To the early Euro-American explorers and settlers these mountains presented formidable obstacles, but the native peoples called them home.

River and Lake Chelan; the *Upper Skagit*, along the Skagit River below the Newhalem Gorge; and the *Nlaka'pamux (Lower Thompson)*, in British Columbia and along the Skagit River above the Newhalem Gorge. This gorge probably acted as a major physical and cultural barrier to prehistoric peoples. Even today it is a barrier; often closed in winter by avalanches, there are no major permanent towns upriver from Newhalem.

What were native peoples doing in the mountains? How did they live? We can gain an understanding of how prehistoric Indians used the landscape of the North Cascades by examining land use in the early historic period and how we use the land today. In addition to permanent residences in the lower river valleys, early inhabitants of the North Cascades used the mountains for three main purposes: travel, trade, and obtaining local resources.

The difficulty of travel across these rugged mountains made intimate knowledge of them extremely important. Routes to the major mountain passes were vital to the Indians. Upper Skagit and Lake Chelan Indians used Cascade Pass regularly as a trade route through the mountains. The

Today, trails lead to many of the high lakes. Indian hunting camps have been found near Juanita Lake in Lake Chelan National Recreation Area. The open slopes near the lake attract many animals including bear, deer, and mountain goat.

Upper Skagit reportedly cached canoes at the head of Lake Chelan to use in their trips southward down the lake. The mountains were inhabited mainly in summer and fall when milder weather and melting snows permitted access into the high country. But reports exist that Cascade Pass might have been traversed in winter by Upper Skagit Indians en route to Lake Chelan. Recent archaeological evidence indicates that Whatcom Pass might have been used by the Chilliwack and Nlaka'pamux (Lower Thompson) Indians as a trade route across the northern end of the range. When traveling to the east, the Chelan Indians crossed by way of Twisp Pass.

Native Americans seeking food and certain scarce resources penetrated deep into the North Cascades in summer. Stone artifacts found on Copper Ridge at an altitude of over 5,000 feet indicate that Indians at this site quarried an obsidian-like stone known as welded tuff, used in making tools. Another quarry site has been discovered along the shores of Ross Lake. There were hunting and gathering activities everywhere in the mountain world. Hunting camps have been found as high as 6,600 feet at Juanita Lake, near War Creek Pass.

Mountain goats were one of the most important animals hunted throughout the North Cascades. Not only were goats hunted for their meat but also for their wool, which possesses great insulating properties. Demand was high, especially among the Salishan-speaking peoples, making goat wool one of the major trade items throughout the region. Goat bones 1,300 years old were found in a rock shelter along Newhalem Creek (*Newhalem* is a Skagit word meaning "goat snare"). This site was most likely a hunting camp or a storage facility rather than a permanent residence.

In addition to mountain goats, Native Americans hunted deer, elk, bear, and marmot. Salmon were especially important to the people living along the Chilliwack River and along the Skagit River below the Newhalem Gorge. The gorge of the Skagit River was a major physical barrier to migrating salmon, which therefore were not a major food resource for the Nlaka'pamux (Lower Thompson) Indians living in what is now North Cascades National Park.

Other important trade goods among North Cascades Indians included dried salmon, stone for toolmaking, berries gathered in the high mountains in the fall, eulachon oil (a high-carbohydrate oil from a small smeltlike fish), and

KEITH GUNNAR

Hikers gaze across the Picket Range from Copper Mountain Lookout. Long used by the U.S. Forest Service as a fire lookout, the cabin is now used as a backcountry patrol cabin by National Park Service Rangers.

hemp (traded from the interior and used for rope and cordage).

Native American cultures changed quickly in the historic period. Smallpox spread rapidly through unresistant and previously unexposed Indian populations, even affecting those who had never seen the colonists. By the time Euro-Americans entered the North Cascades, the diseases of the settlers had already decimated the native populations. Major smallpox epidemics occurred about 1780 and from 1825 to 1835. Even the earliest written records about Native Americans of the North Cascades are records of a dying culture.

The early white explorers and settlers who entered the mountains of the North Cascades lived close to the land much as the Indians did. However, as white populations grew and centralized in villages, and became farmers and importers of food and materials, they became less dependent upon natural cycles of the land.

EXPLORERS AND SETTLERS

All those who have lived in the North Cascades have made use of the many resources here. Commercial exploitation begun by fur trappers of the early nineteenth century was continued by the miners, loggers, and dam builders of the 1900s.

Fur traders, traveling by canoe and foot, were among the first Euro-Americans to venture into

Rainbow Lake lies nestled deep in the backcountry, a reminder that for a wilderness ecosystem to survive it must remain intact. Only if all elements of an ecosystem are preserved can the variety of necessary habitats exist to provide plants, animals, and humans with the space needed to continue to find refuge from the encroaching world of civilization.

the North Cascades wilderness in the late 1700s. Seeking to follow the Columbia River to the Pacific Ocean, these explorers entered only the lower reaches of the North Cascades. The earliest recorded crossing of the North Cascades by a Euro-American occurred in 1814. Alexander Ross, a fur trader, crossed Twisp Pass and descended Bridge Creek to the Stehekin River, which he then followed upstream. Finally crossing Cascade Pass, he traced the Cascade River downstream to its confluence with the Skagit River. Maps of Washington Territory in 1860 show large areas still labeled "unexplored."

Between 1857 and 1859 Henry Custer, a Swiss topographer, surveyed the boundary between Canada (then Great Britain) and the United States along the 49th parallel. His explorations included the watersheds of the Nooksack and Chilliwack rivers, the alpine country around Whatcom Pass and the Picket Range, and the upper Skagit River above Ruby Creek.

Over the next 40 years many expeditions penetrated the heartland of the North Cascades, although these explorers kept to the major river systems and passes. Cascade Pass was crossed for the second time by Euro-Americans in 1877 by the Otto Klement party in their search for gold. In 1882 Lieutenant Henry Pierce was assigned by the U.S. Army to explore the North Cascades region of Washington Territory. His party explored the Stehekin River valley, traversed Cascade Pass after 22 days of travel, and descended the Skagit River to Sedro-Woolley (SEE-dro WOOL-lee). He found gold-bearing quartz west of Cascade Pass in the Eldorado Peak area. While exploration of the mountains continued, settlers began to sink roots into the lush river valleys.

The North Cascades provided formidable barriers to settlement. In 1846 the Territory of Washington opened to homesteading, but it was not until the late 1870s, with the clearing of a massive natural logjam on the Skagit River, that settlers moved upriver. On the east side of the range, homesteaders established claims along the Stehekin River at the head of Lake Chelan.

Settlement along the three major river systems, the Skagit, Cascade, and Stehekin, continued through the 1880s. Marblemount, at the confluence of the Cascade and Skagit rivers, was established as a base for miners; the first wagon road was built into the area in 1892. Early settlers faced many challenges, for the rugged environment made this a harsh land to live in. The majority of early settlers were not farmers but shopkeepers and innkeepers who came to sell goods and services to the trappers and prospectors who ventured up the rivers.

Beavers, bears, wolves, lynx, fishers, martens, and foxes were all sought by trappers in the North Cascades. Trapping was primarily a winter activity—the most difficult season to be afield in the mountains. Many of the early settlers trapped to supplement their income. John

Fur trappers, searching for beaver, were among the first explorers of the North Cascades mountains in the late 1700s.

McMillan, a miner, ran traplines along Big Beaver Creek and the Upper Skagit River in the late nineteenth century.

The story of mining in the North Cascades is one of broken dreams. In the 1850s prospectors began searching for gold along the banks of the Skagit River. After gold was discovered along Ruby Creek in the late 1870s, hundreds of miners swarmed over the upper Skagit valley. They found little gold, and the rush was over by 1880.

Over the few next decades miners turned their attention to other minerals, primarily silver and lead, located higher in the mountains. New claims were established in the high country around Cascade Pass, including Doubtful Lake, Boston and Horseshoe basins, and Bridge Creek. A rich silver deposit was found just below Boston Glacier near the headwaters of Thunder Creek in 1892, and another rush was on. Some silver was located, but the costs of getting the ore out were too high. By 1913 most of the Thunder Creek mining companies had folded. Eventually the combination of short seasons, inhospitable terrain, unpredictable weather, and lack of transportation doomed these ventures to failure.

Many of the hundreds of miners who traveled into the Skagit and Stehekin valleys stayed on after their dreams were shattered. As the miners moved farther into the wilderness they built trails, bridges, tunnels, cabins, and wagon roads. The construction of a miner's trail along the north bank of the Skagit River required dynamiting a

Hikers crossing Cascade Pass today walk on a well-maintained trail, a far cry from the struggles of early Euro-American explorers such as Alexander Ross who first traversed beneath the spires of Magic Mountain in 1814.

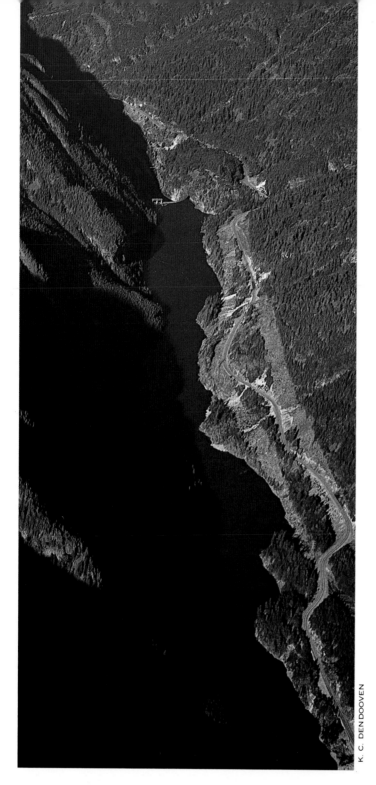

The North Cascades Highway (State Route 20) snakes beside Gorge Lake, the most westerly of three reservoirs along the Skagit River. The present Gorge Dam was completed in 1961, following a diversionary dam built in 1924. The narrow and tortuous path of the Skagit River cut deep gorges through the mountains. Explorers following the river were stopped by the deep gorge between the present towns of Newhalem and Diablo.

Rainy and Washington passes, followed earlier exploration of possible routes through the Picket Range and over Cascade Pass. The North Cascades Highway is passable only during the warmer months. Nature still rules in the North Cascades.

Timber was recognized as one of the major resources of the Cascades at an early date. Once the natural logjams that blocked the lower Skagit were cleared away in the 1870s, logging began to extend into the heart of the mountains. Logs were rafted down the river to be milled at settlements downstream. The lack of an adequate transportation system hindered early efforts to expand logging operations deep into the mountains. By far the most intensive logging that ever took place in the North Cascades occurred during the construction of the Skagit River hydroelectric project in the twentieth century.

The many glacier-fed streams and rivers of the North Cascades have always been recognized as an important resource. The rivers provided the earliest pathways into the mountains, although these tumultuous waters have also hindered travel at times. The first power plant on the Skagit River was constructed in the 1920s by the Davis family at their homestead at Cedar Bar. Their small water wheel was powered by the nearby waters of Stetattle Creek. Similar Pelton wheels were used to produce electric power along Thunder Creek and the Stehekin River.

Construction of major hydroelectic development of the Skagit River began in 1918, when Seattle City Light was issued permits to begin construction of three dams along the river. Seattle City Light eventually built a railroad up the Skagit Valley to its company towns of Newhalem and Diablo. A diversionary dam at Gorge Creek was completed in 1924, and Diablo Dam—at that time the highest dam in the world—in 1930. Ross Dam, dedicated in 1940, was raised in 1949 to 540 feet, making it the highest of the three dams providing power to the city of Seattle. Visible from State Route 20 between Newhalem and Diablo, the present Gorge Dam was completed in 1961.

ledge out of sheer canyon walls and building suspension bridges over open gorges. The Goat Trail had one particularly dangerous section known as the Devil's Corner, where a hanging bridge made of split logs traversed a narrow ledge. Roads were built up the Cascade River and along the Stehekin River from Bridge Creek to what is now Cottonwood Camp.

It was not until 1972, with the completion of the North Cascades Highway (State Route 20) across Rainy and Washington passes, that a modern road traversed the North Cascades. Construction of this highway, which follows the Skagit River to Ruby Creek, then veers to cross

Under the fresh blanket of a December storm, McGregor Mountain reaches into a clearing sky. In winter the high country is quiet. Most of the animals have departed for the valleys, or hibernate beneath the snow.

NORTH CASCADES NATIONAL PARK

In order to preserve for the benefit, use, and inspiration of present and future generations certain majestic mountain scenery, snowfields, glaciers, alpine meadows, and other unique natural features in the North Cascade Mountains of the State of Washington, there is hereby established . . . the North Cascades National Park.
    —*North Cascades Act of 1968*

The magnificent wilderness mountains of the North Cascades have been admired for generations. In 1897 much of the area was removed from public domain and managed as part of the Washington Forest Reserve. In 1924 this became part of Mount Baker National Forest (later Mount Baker–Snoqualmie National Forest). The idea of a North Cascades National Park was first proposed by the Mazama Outing Club of Portland, Oregon, in 1906. There had been an earlier proposal, in 1892, for a park along Lake Chelan in order to save the dwindling population of mountain goats.

Controversy arose over the appropriate use of wild lands, with various factions favoring protection or resource exploitation. Continuing public pressure led to the North Cascades Act, passed by the Ninetieth Congress and signed by President Lyndon B. Johnson on October 2, 1968. It created North Cascades National Park Service Complex, comprising 684,000 acres of wild lands, including the park's north and south units, as well as Ross Lake and Lake Chelan national recreation areas. This same act created the adjacent Pasayten Wilderness of 505,000 acres and enlarged the Glacier Peak Wilderness to 464,000 acres.

SUGGESTED READING

BECKEY, FRED. *Challenge of the North Cascades.* Seattle, Washington: The Mountaineers, 1969.

COLLINS, JUNE M. *Valley of the Spirits: The Upper Skagit Indians of Western Washington.* Seattle: University of Washington Press, 1974.

JENKING, WILL D. *Last Frontier in the North Cascades.* Skagit County Historical Society, Skagit Historical Series No. 8. Mount Vernon, Washington: 1984.

PITZER, PAUL C. *Building the Skagit: A Century of Upper Skagit Valley History.* Portland, Oregon: The Galley Press, 1978.

ROE, JOANN. *The North Cascadians.* Seattle, Washington: Madrona Publishers, 1980.

Climbers have always been attracted to the rugged mountains of the North Cascades. Here mountaineers look for safe passages through the deep crevasses of the Challenger Glacier. With ice ax, rope, crampons, and skill, travel through this icy wilderness is safe for the experienced mountaineer.

BOB & IRA SPRING

North Cascades Today: The Challenge of Wilderness

North Cascades is a young park lying in the heart of young mountains. The park forms the core of a vast wilderness, perhaps the wildest place left in the contiguous United States. Surrounding lands include Mount Baker–Snoqualmie, Okanogan, and Wenatchee national forests; and Glacier Peak, Pasayten, Mount Baker, Lake Chelan-Sawtooth, Boulder River, Noisy-Diobsud, and Henry M. Jackson wilderness areas.

You can wander forever through the North Cascades and always see new mountains and new vistas endlessly unfolding. During an autumn storm half-seen peaks lie shrouded in mist, green walls cut by slender threads of falling water. It is a land of mystery and magic.

The North Cascades provide a place where people can go to experience nature on her own terms, a place where all the artifacts of modern technological civilization fall away. We are left standing alone, just below the summit, mist rising from the forest below; before us there is nothing but an endless sea of peaks.

For a climber perched on a narrow, ice-covered ledge, high on the north face of Forbidden Peak, the challenge of wilderness is real and immediate. It speaks to the love of wild places, of freedom, of dealing directly with nature on her own terms. For the fisherman trying to drop a fly over a swirling eddy in the headwaters of Granite Creek the challenge is similar—although perhaps not as fraught with consequences. But what of the day hiker, the car camper, the picnicker, the family out for an afternoon walk? How does the wilderness world of the North Cascades speak to them?

It has been said that wilderness is a state of mind, that participants bring their own expectations to wild lands, seeking to be surprised and

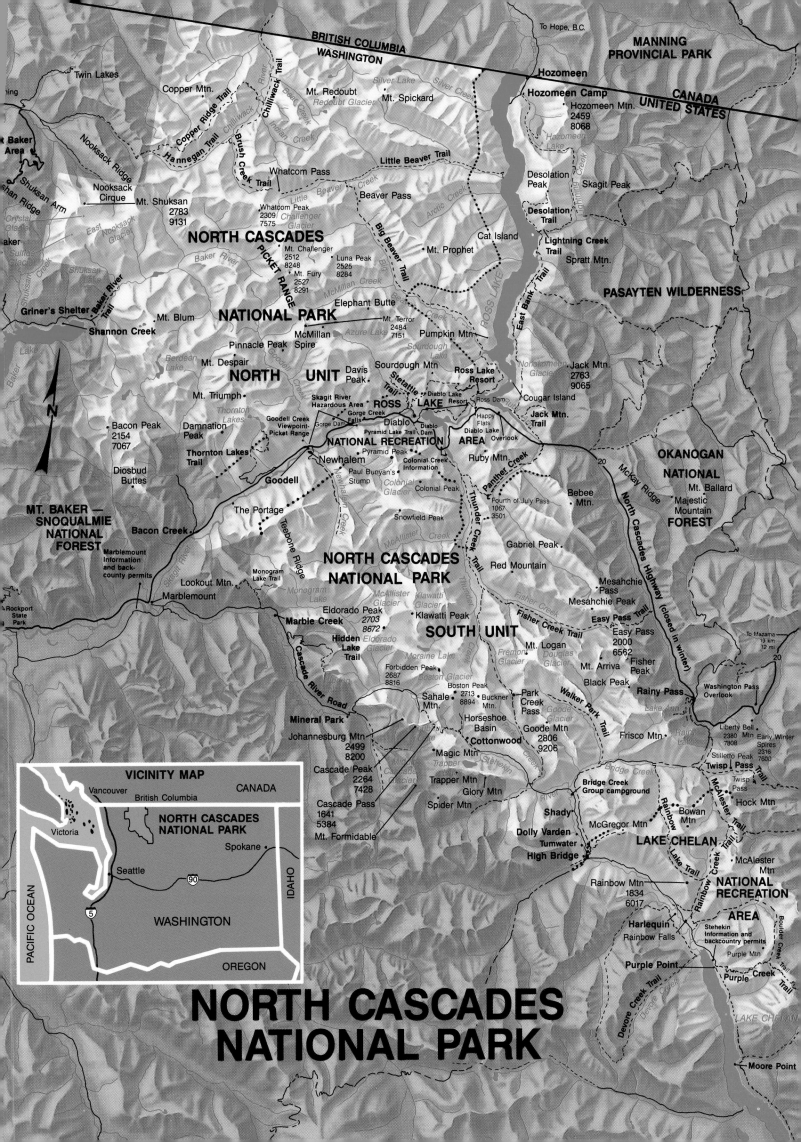

NORTH CASCADES
NATIONAL PARK

awakened to something new. All visitors to the North Cascades experience its wild power in their own ways. As the numbers of people coming to the North Cascades increase, they bring with them a new challenge—how to maintain the quality of the very wilderness they are seeking.

There are two paradoxes inherent in the mandate given to the National Park Service to manage the wild lands of the North Cascades. The first of these is to provide simultaneously for preservation and use—to protect the land for future generations while allowing present generations to experience its beauty and magic. The second paradox is that management, by its very nature, implies control, something that is alien to the wilderness experience.

It was not until 1963 that a pair of experienced and adventurous mountaineers made the first alpine traverse of the Picket Range. This remote and isolated range, the very heart of the North Cascades wilderness, now hosts many climbing parties each summer. The isolation and solitude of the wilderness are diminishing. Are the wilderness values that we seek in the mountain lands being threatened by our own presence and numbers?

North Cascades National Park is grappling with these difficult questions. To preserve the fragile alpine vegetation many of the subalpine passes have been closed to camping. Campfires are prohibited except in designated areas. An active program of plant restoration is repairing damage to the high country. Native subalpine plants grown in a lowland greenhouse in Marblemount are transplanted into the mountains in the fall. These are attempts to preserve the wilderness, to teach new wilderness ethics, and to speak of the value of wild places for their own sake as well as ours.

The essence of the North Cascades wilderness—this land of rock and ice and jagged peaks—lies far away from the roads and campgrounds, up high in the cold mountain air, where solitude and silence speak louder than the wind.

The glow of sunset behind Mount Shuksan gives promise of new explorations in the morning.

PAT O'HARA

Books on National Park areas in "The Story Behind the Scenery" series are: Acadia, Alcatraz Island, Arches, Badlands, Big Bend, Biscayne, Blue Ridge Parkway, Bryce Canyon, Canyon de Chelly, Canyonlands, Cape Cod, Capitol Reef, Channel Islands, Civil War Parks, Colonial, Crater Lake, Death Valley, Denali, Devils Tower, Dinosaur, Everglades, Fort Clatsop, Gettysburg, Glacier, Glen Canyon-Lake Powell, Grand Canyon, Grand Canyon-North Rim, Grand Teton, Great Basin, Great Smoky Mountains, Haleakalā, Hawai`i Volcanoes, Independence, Joshua Tree, Lake Mead-Hoover Dam, Lassen Volcanic, Lincoln Parks, Mammoth Cave, Mesa Verde, Mount Rainier, Mount Rushmore, Mount St. Helens, National Park Service, National Seashores, North Cascades, Olympic, Petrified Forest, Redwood, Rocky Mountain, Scotty's Castle, Sequoia & Kings Canyon, Shenandoah, Statue of Liberty, Theodore Roosevelt, Virgin Islands, Yellowstone, Yosemite, Zion.

Additional books in "The Story Behind the Scenery" series are: Annapolis, Big Sur, California Gold Country, California Trail, Colorado Plateau, Columbia River Gorge, Fire: A Force of Nature, Grand Circle Adventure, John Wesley Powell, Kauai, Lake Tahoe, Las Vegas, Lewis & Clark, Monument Valley, Mormon Temple Square, Mormon Trail, Mount St. Helens, Nevada's Red Rock Canyon, Nevada's Valley of Fire, Oregon Trail, Oregon Trail Center, Santa Catalina, Santa Fe Trail, Sharks, Sonoran Desert, U.S. Virgin Islands, Water: A Gift of Nature, Whales.

Call (800-626-9673), fax (702-433-3420), or write to the address below.

Published by KC Publications, 3245 E. Patrick Ln., Suite A, Las Vegas, NV 89120.

Inside back cover: Adrift in a sea of clouds, the summits of the North Cascades reach toward an evening sky. Photo by John Dittli

Back cover: Pelton Basin and Pelton Peak, looking east from Cascade Pass. Photo by Charles Gurche

Created, Designed, and Published in the U.S.A.
Printed by Doosan Dong-A Co., Ltd., Seoul, Korea
Paper produced exclusively by Hankuk Paper Mfg. Co., Ltd.